HOW TO WRITE MINUTES

"Our recording secretary has asked that she be excused from keeping the minutes of our meetings as she can never figure out what's going on."

How To Write Minutes

MIGNON CASSELBERRY

John Daniel, Publisher
SANTA BARBARA
1986

To D. Rajagopal
with love and gratitude.

LIBRARY OF CONGRESS CATALOGING-IN-PUBLICATION DATA
Casselberry, Mignon, 1908–
HOW TO WRITE MINUTES.
1. Meetings—Handbooks, manuals, etc.
2. Seminars—Handbooks, manuals, etc.
3. Corporate minutes—Handbooks, manuals, etc.
I. Title.
AS6.C33   1986   658.4'563   86.16793
ISBN 0–936784–21–0 (PBK)

Published by
JOHN DANIEL, PUBLISHER
Post Office Box 21922
Santa Barbara, California 93121

Table of Contents

Note: In this manual, the term "Secretary" is used also to indicate a Recording Secretary.

FOREWORD

FEW BUSINESS CORPORATIONS and fewer voluntary associations or eleemosynary institutions have professional secretaries to take and to keep the minutes. In most organizations, the office of secretary often becomes difficult to fill owing to the apprehension that the task of a secretary is at once demanding, unrewarding, unimportant and formalistic. Mrs. Casselberry's handbook is a practical guide which not only meets but also dispels these common misconceptions.

The handbook distinguishes formalism from consistent format. It urges that each organization select a format suited to the nature of the organization and that care be taken to apply the selected format consistently and reliably. In exchange, it suggests that secretaries dispense with the frequently frustrating attempt to mimic rigid, legalistic styles with which few persons, other than lawyers, feel comfortable. This is a formula by which most persons with a will to do so can achieve consistent, concise and clear recording of the action of the organization.

This handbook will be of use alike to persons who have discharged the duties of secretaries and to those who have never held the office. It should be a handbook that organizations keep with the minutes book. The handbook describes the concepts with which a secretary must be familiar and examines the tools the secretary must use in order to be effective at the job. The conclusions are grounded on the long experience of the author both in taking and keeping minutes properly and in reviewing, correcting, and researching minutes taken by less able secretaries.

Perhaps most importantly, the handbook explains that the taking and keeping of minutes is not a meaningless formality but is rather the creation of a document which is a guide to the present activities of the organization and which eventually becomes its history. Thus, the care, or carelessness, with which the job is done will be, along with the resolutions, recorded permanently.

Once the importance of the job is appreciated, the tangible rewards of doing it well are manifest. But it seems clear that Mrs. Casselberry would wish that persons who find her book useful would derive the greatest satisfaction, as she does, from the knowledge of having made a meaningful contribution to the goals of the organization of which the secretary can be so important a part.

—J.A. URIBE, lawyer
Los Angeles, California

1. The Secretary

THE OFFICE OF Secretary is arduous in terms of clerical work and time required. The office requires a high degree of responsibility, dependably continuous attendance at meetings, some business experience, and education.

2. Language Of Minutes

USE SIMPLE, ORDINARY words which are commonly understood. When precision is important and the ideas complex, use the words which exactly convey the meaning. Use a dictionary and a thesaurus when necessary. The purpose of the words is to convey an idea. The idea must first be clear in your own mind before you try to convey it.*

Sophisticated legalistic language is difficult to understand by all of us who are not lawyers. So do not try to write in "legalese." Any lawyer can understand clear, precise, simple language, should your minutes ever have to be interpreted in litigation.

Do not imitate some old traditional, formal business expressions you may have heard. They are not superior to clear, accurate, contemporary style.

Write in complete sentences (not phrases or clauses joined by dashes). If you are not a good writer, teach yourself to be one. If you do not already have them, acquire and use a dictionary, a thesaurus, and a text or secretary's handbook on English usage. Expand your vocabulary. Learn punctuation. Learn the correct use of a semicolon, a dash, an apostrophe, and the correct division of words into syllables. Enjoy the opportunity to improve yourself.

---

*Do not think this too obvious to mention; I have read and heard minutes written by a secretary who had no idea what was the topic under discussion, but too embarrassed to admit it. If you do not comprehend what is going on at a certain point in a meeting, of course, you cannot report it. Before reporting on that item you will need to discuss with the Chairman what happened.

3. Minutes

THE MINUTES OF a meeting state:

1. Whether the meeting was a regular, special, annual or adjourned meeting;
2. Name of the organization;
3. Address of place meeting was held;
4. For what hour called, and time actually called to order;
5. Names and titles of officers present;
6. Names of those present if a small group such as a Board of Directors or Trustees; if a larger group, a note of approximately the number present;
7. If the group is a Committee or Board with a limited number of members, a list of those absent;
8. Names of invited guests or special speakers present.

If the practice of signing waivers is followed (see page 22), the waiver is presented and signed as soon as the meeting is opened; mention of this action is made in the minutes as follows:

> The Chairman announced that this meeting was being held pursuant to a written waiver of notice thereof and consent thereto signed by all the directors (or trustees) of the corporation. Such waiver and consent was presented to the meeting, and upon motion duly made, seconded and unanimously passed was made a part of the records of the meeting and now precedes the minutes of this meeting in the minutes book of the corporation.

Except for the waiver, the first item to be taken up is the approval of the minutes of the last meeting. If the minutes were not already mailed out after the previous meeting, they are usually read aloud at this point and corrected if need be. Then a resolution is passed approving them.

A satisfactory procedure in many instances is for the Secretary to write the minutes as soon as convenient after a meeting, marking the minutes at the top of the first page as "A draft subject to correction at the next meeting" and mailing them to each director with a notice of the next meeting attached thereto. The Secretary can then type the minutes in permanent form after correction and approval. Advantages to this procedure include that the minutes are written while memories are fresh and that those who have received instructions or who have agreed to do certain business before the next meeting are thereby reminded to do so. The minutes book will be kept neat without handwritten corrections. Also, the minutes will not need reading at the subsequent meeting; a resolution can be passed approving them "as mailed out" or "as mailed out and corrected." This saves time at a meeting.

The reading of the minutes can be postponed if there is a compelling reason for doing so, but this practice eliminates the very purpose of minutes—which is to keep an up-to-date and accurate record of activities.

Old business should be taken up before considering new business. Conversations or subject matter may become confused or mixed in time or logical sequence, but the Secretary should write the minutes in proper sequence, putting in one paragraph all decisions about a topic regardless of when in the meeting the action or comment occurred. The less competent the Chairperson, the more work for the Secretary!

Minutes should only record new, additional information, not repeat anything previously mentioned. They should record chiefly *actions taken* and not discussions. The writing should be precise and compact, omitting all insignificant details.

Sometimes visitors are invited to a meeting to enter into a discussion or to impart information. The Secretary need not record all that is said under such circumstances, but should make note of the name and title of the visitor, the purpose of his being there, and the subject and general significance of the visitor's remarks.

If a vital disagreement divides the directors in a significant manner, the Secretary should record this briefly by mentioning the opposing views in an objective way, but without going into any lengthy description.

It is necessary for a Secretary to be completely objective. If the Secretary is personally involved in a matter of disagreement, or is a member of another body with whom business is being transacted, he or she becomes disqualified and should resign as an officer from one or the other organization.

Serious matters of continuing interest discussed but not resolved at a meeting and certain to come before the group for further discussion or a final decision later (such as planning the construction of a building), need not be recorded in detail and need not even be mentioned unless new information has been brought in.

Copies of extremely significant documents referred to in a discussion should be obtained by the Secretary and put into the minutes book. The pages of the minutes book are numbered as added, and appended material is not numbered but marked at the top "to follow page — ," and, at the point the appended material is mentioned within the minutes, reference should be made by the expression "(appended hereto)."

It is useful to give a title to each paragraph and to type it near the outside edge of the paper, left edge of a sheet on the left side of the book and right edge of a sheet on the right side of the book. This greatly helps when looking back over the record for information on actions or discussions. (See page 32-34 for illustration.)

If the date of the next meeting is set, it should be recorded just before the resolution for adjournment, with which every meeting should close. The Secretary records who makes the resolution, who seconds it, etc., and the time of closing. Signature lines are provided for the Secretary and for the Chairman.

4. Action

"ACTION" REFERS TO a decision reached by a deliberating group which is binding because it has been formally stated and agreed to either *unanimously* or by a *majority* (more than half) or some other proportion of those present as required by the By-Laws (such as a *two-thirds majority*).

All "actions" are recorded as resolutions.

Resolutions form the guidelines and boundaries for the conduct of business. A resolution must be conformed to and abided by after its adoption until such time as it is changed or rescinded by another resolution.

There may be resolutions for other purposes, too, such as:

(1) Directing a certain person to take certain action on behalf of the group. (Examples: sign papers, open a bank account, negotiate a loan, conduct an escrow, confer with a broker, inquire about property, consummate a purchase);

(2) Expressing gratitude to a person for assistance or services performed. (Examples: a retiring officer, trustee, director, member, visitor, speaker, entertainer).

5. The Resolution

A RESOLUTION IS THE formal expression of a decision, an attitude, a plan, an opinion, or the will of a deliberating group. When adopted by vote, it constitutes "action" and is to be carried out according to its directives, within the procedural framework of the By-Laws.

The Secretary must, when writing the minutes, phrase the motion in the proper form of a resolution, however inadequately the maker of the motion states it. Sometimes resolutions to be proposed at a meeting are written out and provided to the directors before or at a meeting, a commendable practice which expedites the conduct of the meeting by having the proposal in writing before each director at the time of discussion. The Secretary must observe at the time of voting whether any change has been made in the pre-written resolution.

Resolutions proposed "from the floor," meaning that there is not a pre-written statement of the proposed resolution, require that the Secretary understand what is said. Such action is often fast and poorly stated from the point of view of written language usage and the Secretary must determine what was *meant,* which is sometimes not exactly what is said, and put it into good written form. The Secretary must therefore be a good listener and a good writer. (See Section 2)

To be "brought before the house," that is, to be presented for consideration and voting, the resolution must have the initial support of at least two persons, one who "makes the motion" (states the proposed resolution) and another who, also in favor of the proposed action, "seconds" the proposed resolution. The Chairman then presents it to the assembly for questioning, discussing and voting. Those opposed to the resolution may then express their opinions, thus having an opportunity to inform the assembly and influence the opinions of the others present. To be adopted or "passed" it must receive as great a proportion of favorable votes as are required by the By-Laws, or, in any event, a majority (more than half) of the votes. (See page 30.) The resolution will be defeated unless the required number of "yes" votes are cast, and, if so, the matter is dismissed. The Secretary records only that "a proposed resolution in the matter of _____ was defeated."

If there is no "second" to a proposed resolution, it dies then and there and there is no discussion or voting on it.

Samples of Resolutions

UNANIMOUS
APPROVAL

Upon motion of Mr. Baker, seconded by Mrs. Edwards and unanimously passed, it was

Resolved that this association (club, body, assembly, corporation, board or whatever) does hereby extend its thanks to Supervisor James McDonald for attending our meeting on May 16 last, and explaining the flood-control problems of the county, and be it Further Resolved that the President, (name), be and he is hereby requested to write a letter of appreciation to Mr. McDonald, informing him of the passage of this resolution.

APPROVAL
WITH AN
ABSTENTION

Upon motion of Mr. Maguire, seconded by Miss Halton, Mr. Babcock abstaining, all others in favor, it was
Resolved that the proposed budget

for (dates of period of time) be and it is hereby approved as presented.

APPROVAL
WITH
OPPOSITION

Upon motion of Mrs. Field, seconded by Mr. Zabrosky, twenty-six (26) in favor, twelve (12) opposed, it was
Resolved that this organization

enter a float in the July 4 parade being sponsored by the Chamber of Commerce. (See also sample resolution under "Resolutions Regarding Property," page 18.)

However long and complex a resolution may have to be, it is nevertheless *one* sentence and should be so constructed and punctuated. Example:

A RESOLUTION IS A SENTENCE

WHEREAS the funds required for the maintenance and operation of the Elm Grove Sanitary District are received from service charges for the use of the Elm Grove sewer collection and treatment facilities, and

WHEREAS said services are billed by the office staff of the Elm Grove Sanitary District bimonthly on or about the first day of January, March, May, July, September, and November of each year, each bimonthly billing covering services rendered for the preceding month and the services to be rendered during the month of billing, and

WHEREAS a large number of said bills are unpaid, and

WHEREAS it now appears to the Board of Directors of the Elm Grove Sanitary District that rules and regulations governing the time for payment and penalty for delinquent payments are needed, therefore be it now

RESOLVED that bimonthly bills for sewer collection and treatment services furnished by Elm Grove Sanitary District shall be due and payable on receipt of the bimonthly billing and shall become delinquent if not paid on or before the 10th day of the month following the bimonthly billing period, and be it

FURTHER RESOLVED that on and after September 1, 1977, all bills for sewer collection and treatment services not paid on or before the 10th day of the month following the end of the billing period shall be charged a basic penalty of ten percent (10%) for nonpayment of the charges for services rendered, provided, however, that if the 10th day of the month following the last day of the billing period falls on a Saturday, Sunday or legal holiday, the penalty shall not take effect until the day following the next business day, and be it

FURTHER RESOLVED that a basic penalty of ten percent (10%) for nonpayment of the charges for services rendered for any period ending on or before July 31, 1977, shall be charged if said bills are not paid on or before October 21, 1977, and be it

FURTHER RESOLVED that all previous regulations in conflict with this resolution be and they are hereby repealed.

RESOLUTIONS   Sometimes banks, escrow companies,
REQUIRED   government regulatory agencies and
BY OTHERS   others require certain resolutions for
                     which they provide the wording.
Instead of entering their entire wording into the minutes, the following type of resolution can be passed and a printed copy of the required resolution, which is provided by the agency requiring it, is appended to the minutes (also see page 15, 19):

Upon motion of Ms. Huffner, seconded by Mr. Allen and unanimously passed, it was

RESOLVED that the form of resolution required by the First Western National Bank of a corporation desiring to borrow money be and it is hereby approved, and be it

FURTHER RESOLVED that a copy of said resolution be appended to the minutes of this meeting, and be it

FURTHER RESOLVED that the President, (name), and Secretary, (name), of this corporation be and they are hereby authorized to execute on behalf of this corporation any and all documents required to consummate this loan.

RESOLUTIONS   Upon motion of Mr. Grimes, seconded
REGARDING   by Mr. Stockman, Mr. Field and Miss
PROPERTY   Gleason opposed, all others in favor, it
                     was

RESOLVED that this corporation undertake to purchase the property commonly known heretofore as the Federal Office Building at (full address) and be it

FURTHER RESOLVED that the President, (name), and Secretary, (name), be and they are hereby requested and authorized to inquire on behalf of this corporation into the possibility of such a purchase and its attendant obligations, and be it

FURTHER RESOLVED that (name of Secretary) be and (she or he) is hereby requested to make a full report at the next meeting of the findings in this connection.

Upon motion of Mrs. Nicholas, seconded by Mr. Mitchell and unanimously passed, it was

RESOLVED that the unimproved property located at 216 East Main Street (City, County and State) and more particularly described in the deed thereto, now owned by this corporation be listed for sale for a period of three months with a licensed broker for a price of not less than (amount), and be it

FURTHER RESOLVED that the President, (name), and Secretary, (name), be and they are hereby authorized to contact a suitable broker, enter into negotiations, and sign all documents on behalf of this corporation in order to execute and consummate the listing.

Upon motion of Miss Garcia, sec- **RESOLUTION**
onded by Mrs. Carter and passed by **BY SHOWING**
an overwhelming majority as indicated **OF HANDS**
by a showing of hands, it was

RESOLVED that this association go on record as being in favor of reinstituting the mid-morning milk-and-crackers program for elementary school children, and be it

FURTHER RESOLVED that the Secretary, (name), be and (she or he) is hereby requested so to inform the President of the Board of the Unified School District of (name of area or town).

Sometimes a matter is brought up or a **ACTION BY**
resolution proposed which invokes a **ACCLAMATION**
so obviously unanimous favorable
response that no vote need be taken; it can then be recorded that the matter was settled (or the resolution passed) by *acclamation*.

Another kind of solution to a question **SENSE OF**
sometimes occurs when a discussion **A MEETING**
brings out the fact that there is general
agreement, but no formal resolution is required; it can then be recorded:

"Regarding the matter of _____, the sense of the meeting was that _____."

When it becomes necessary to rescind **RESCINDING**
action previously taken, a new resolu- **ACTION**
tion must be passed making this clear.
The Secretary should write the new resolution regarding the mat-

ter in unmistakably clear language, referring within the text of the new resolution to the first resolution by date and page number in the Minutes Book. The Secretary should also annotate in red ink the original resolution by writing in the margin "Rescinded (date), see page—."

The reference titles of the paragraphs should be similar in wording so that it is easy to identify the related items.

Example:

FEDERAL OFFICE BUILDING — RESOLVED that this corporation undertake to purchase the property commonly known heretofore as the Federal Office Building at 600 Forest Avenue, Hagerstown, North Dakota, and be it

FURTHER RESOLVED that the President, A.J. Wilton, and Secretary, Mary Elmwood, be and they are hereby requested and authorized to inquire on behalf of this corporation into the possibility of such [etc.]

Excerpt from Minutes of March 15, 1977 showing resolution which was rescinded June 15, 1977, this page in the Minutes Book being so marked by hand in red.

FEDERAL OFFICE BUILDING — RESOLVED that the resolution passed March 15, 1977 (p. 66) to initiate inquiry into the possible purchase by this corporation of the property commonly known heretofore as the Federal Office Building be and it is hereby rescinded.

Excerpt from Minutes of June 15, 1977 showing resolution rescinding a resolution passed at the March 15, 1977 meeting. Note that paragraph identification is the same on both.

There cannot be such a thing as a   **A MEETING**
meeting by mail (obviously a contra-   **BY MAIL**
diction in terms) but ACTION can be
taken by mail without a physical meeting of the Board members
by posting to each member in writing a proposed resolution sub-
mitted and seconded by two members.

If there is unanimity, and signatures indicating affirmation to
the resolution are returned to the Secretary showing that all agree
to the action, this can be recorded in the Minutes Book as action
as binding as any occurring in a meeting.

[This cannot be done, of course, if there is any disapproval.]

6. Notices and Waivers

THE SECRETARY SHOULD mail notices or otherwise announce meetings in accordance with the regulations in the By-Laws.

WAIVER
OF NOTICE

A "Waiver of Notice and Consent to Holding a Meeting (date, time, and place)," when properly signed by *all* directors, can preclude any argument as to the legality of a meeting. It is often used even when written notices have been mailed.

It is typed on a separate sheet (not numbered) and placed in the Minutes Book just before the minutes of the meeting it refers to.

A satisfactory form is as follows:

> We, the undersigned, being all of the members of the Board
> of Trustees (or Directors or whatever) of the (organization's
> name) do hereby declare that we waive notice and consent to
> the holding of a (kind of) meeting of the Board of Trustees
> on (date), at the hour of (time set) at (address, town, state).

There follow signature lines with the names typed under the lines.

This form of waiver can be written separately in the first person and provided to an individual unable to attend. When signed and returned, it is fastened into the Minute Book on the same sheet as the original waiver, thus insuring that *all* directors have signed.

For mention of the waiver in the minutes, see page 11.

ANNUAL
MEETING

If the By-Laws require at least one meeting a year, that is the Annual Meeting. The By-Laws usually state the month in which it should occur. However, it can be postponed. Therefore, a written notice sent by mail to all directors is essential.

A meeting planned for the date and month required by the By-Laws is a "regular" meeting; if it does not occur when required by the By-Laws it is a "special" meeting and the notice should state that the special meeting is "in lieu of the (month) meeting." In the case of an Annual Meeting, the notice should state that it is a notice of the "annual Meeting for 1978." If it has been postponed into the next calendar year, then it is imperative that the notice state that it is the notice of "a Special Meeting in lieu of the Annual Meeting for the Year 1977" even though the date of the meeting will be in the next calendar year (1978).

Examples:

LOMA VISTA PROPERTY OWNERS ASSOC.
Belville, California
NOTICE OF A REGULAR MEETING
March 15, 1978
Monday Evening 7:00 P.M.
at the
Elementary School

EVEREADY RESEARCH FOUNDATION
Compton, Kansas
NOTICE OF A SPECIAL MEETING
IN LIEU OF THE
ANNUAL MEETING FOR THE YEAR 1977
January 15, 1978
Saturday Morning, 10:00 A.M.
at the Research Center, Room 10

---

7. Quorum

QUORUM The minimum number of directors required to be present to conduct business is called a "quorum" and the By-Laws generally state that number. The Chairman and the Secretary should always determine whether a quorum is present. If quorum is not established, then the *only* action which can be taken is to adjourn the meeting to another time by vote of majority of the directors present.

ADJOURNED MEETING Besides the above example, an Adjourned Meeting can also be one continued from a previous occasion when there had not been time to complete the business.

8. The Proxy

A PROXY IS a formal written statement of the transfer of the power to vote from one member of an organization to another. It is addressed by a member not expecting to attend a particular meeting to another member who is expecting to attend. The proxies may be sent to the Secretary to hold, or to the person designated to vote for the absent member. The formality of this procedure depends on the size of the group. In any event, the Secretary must receive the proxy before or during the meeting. The wording for the proxy form may be provided in the By-Laws. (See samples below.) The Secretary should provide such forms to the members. If an attending member holds a proxy or proxies for absent members, this fact should be made known at the time of the voting.

Large commercial corporations usually have a system for obtaining proxies by mail. Smaller organizations may not have established any specific system or form. It is important for an organization to be able to obtain proxies, especially if its meetings are infrequent and its members spread over a large geographical area.

By-Laws usually state what proportion of the membership constitutes a quorum (see pages 24 and 30) and to prevent a failure to reach quorum, proxies are obtained before meetings. If a person who expected to miss a meeting and sent in a proxy later does attend, his proxy is usually automatically cancelled. It is the duty of the Secretary to attend to obtaining the proxies and recording them for use in calculating votes.

In small organizations, and especially in Boards of nonprofit, eleemosynary corporations, it is considered important that trustees (or directors if so called) be present at all meetings for the reason that it is the combined wisdom of their attentive deliberations that is most valuable to the corporation. The use of proxies, if not specifically denied by the By-Laws, is nevertheless frowned upon, as contrary to the best interests of the corporation and the public.

Samples of Proxy Forms:

(Name of Organization)
PROXY FORM

The undersigned hereby appoints (can be more than one) _____ and each of them, his proxy, with power of substitution, to vote at the (regular, special, or annual) __ meeting to be held (date) __ and any adjournments, for (a) the election of trustees (or directors), (b) the election of officers, and (c) all such other business as may properly come before the meeting.

Date _____   Signature _____

(Name of Organization)
PROXY FOR ......* Meeting of Directors
(Date)

KNOW ALL MEN BY THESE PRESENTS that the undersigned hereby constitutes and appoints __ the lawful attorney, agent and proxy of the undersigned with power of substitution, for and in the name, place and stead of the undersigned, to vote and otherwise represent the undersigned at the _____ * meeting of the members of (Name of Organization) to be held at (City, County, State) _____ on (Date) _____, and at any adjournments thereof, for the transaction of any and all business that may come before the meeting with the same powers as the undersigned would possess if the undersigned were personally present.

It is understood that if the undersigned be present at said meeting and elects to vote in person, the powers of the proxyholder herein named will be suspended.

Date _____   Signature _____

*regular, special, or annual

9. The Minutes Book

MINUTES ARE MOST properly kept in a hard-bound, sturdy looseleaf binder manufactured for the purpose. Such binders are available at large stationery stores and are supplied with paper of high quality suitable for both typewriting and handwriting. The paper is often attractively watermarked on the edges. Some binders come with index sheets for "Articles of Incorporation," "By-Laws," and other useful titles.

Much less costly binders can be contrived, however, from ordinary materials such as theme binders, "filler" paper (ruled or unruled), index tabs and so on.

An orderly system of keeping the minutes should be adopted and adhered to except for improvements. The system should not be changed except to *improve* it and an explanatory memorandum of the change and the reason for it should be entered on a separate sheet in the Minutes Book.

If the organization is old enough to have filled more than one Minutes Book, each volume should be clearly and neatly identified (as to dates included) on the first sheet in the book, on the outside of the cover, and on the spine.

The sheets or pages should be numbered front to back as in any book. The practice of putting the most recent minutes in the front wastes space and precludes the numbering of pages which is important for reference purposes. Inasmuch as some of the chief purposes of writing and keeping minutes are to facilitate research into the history of the organization and to refer to actions taken in the past, recent or distant, it is important to follow the system of recording established in the beginning. Whimsical variations in the order of the pages, for example, can create over the years a most disorderly condition of the records and make it difficult to locate data needed for current business.

If, as Secretary of an organization which has been in existence for some time, you receive a disordered Minutes Book, you are certainly entitled to make appropriate changes, but do examine the previous minutes books to see if perhaps an earlier secretary may have used another system which may have been interrupted or neglected. It would be better to restore a satisfactory old system than to start something new which might not be superior after all.

If you are the first Secretary of an organization, take the trouble to find out the best style of Minutes Book which the organization can afford. Set up the best possible system of keeping minutes and consistently use it. Remember that most organizations last many years, perhaps several generations, and eventually there will perhaps be many books on a shelf in a safe or office which will look best and be most useful if consistent in size and binding, and clearly labeled on the outside as to volume number and dates covered.

OFFICERS &   The Minutes Book should include on
DIRECTORS   a separate looseleaf sheet at the begin-
                    ning, for the convenience of the Secre-
tary, a current list of officers and directors, their addresses and telephone numbers. The Minutes Book should likewise include a current list of the directors' names in the order of the date of the end of their terms of office, thus:

DIRECTOR'S NAME	TERM ENDS AT THE END OF THE ANNUAL MEETING OF THE YEAR
James H. Fisher	1979
Emily S. Turner	1979
(Vacant)	1980
John G. Carter	1980
William T. Grimes	1981
Florence E. Stockman	1981
George A. Baker	1981

The Minutes Book should always contain copies of the current By-Laws (see page 30) and the Articles of Incorporation (see page 31).

10. An Executive Committee

IF THE BY-LAWS permit or prescribe the formation of an Executive Committee and the Chairman appoints one, minutes must be kept of its proceedings, but not necessarily by the Secretary of the organization. Copies of such minutes must be filed in the Minutes Book of the organization and reported on at the next meeting of the directors.

The Executive Committee usually has broad powers with specific limitations listed in the By-Laws.

The purpose of the Executive Committee is to expedite many details of business which do not require attention from all the members, or which cannot await the assembling of the entire Board, but are of too great importance to be undertaken by the President alone.

11. By-Laws

BY-LAWS ARE the regulations adopted early in the life of an organization to facilitate the orderly and consistent conduct of its business. They include the terms and conditions of membership, times and frequency of meetings, qualifications and powers of officers, trustees or directors, conduct of elections, and other details pertinent to the nature of the business and purposes of the organization. The By-Laws contain lastly an Article stating how the By-Laws may be changed. A copy of the current By-Laws should be kept in the Minutes Book at all times. Former By-Laws with the dates of their effectiveness should be on file together with a memorandum of the dates of the changes.

There should be kept on hand a number of copies of the By-Laws neatly typed. The Secretary should be ready to provide a copy to the officers, to governmental agencies, or others who have a right to request them.

It is one duty of the Secretary to be thoroughly familiar with the By-Laws so that if there is no Parliamentarian, the Secretary can "watch-dog" the conduct and procedure of business and thus help the Chairman if a decision about procedure has to be made during a meeting. Informal discussion, especially in meetings of small groups, often occurs after a motion has been seconded and the trend of procedure may be momentarily lost; the Secretary can assist the Chairman, if requested to do so, by pointing out where the procedure is at the moment.

The reason for formality in procedure is to make clear the intentions of the membership. A Parliamentarian can help to maintain correct procedure and thus speed up deliberations and discussions, but this office is much neglected these days. The Secretary, who would otherwise be merely a recorder, should be prepared to assist with knowledge of order if there is no parliamentarian.

Chairmen vary in skill in conducting meetings. The President is usually the Chairman and Presidents are sometimes elected for reasons other than suitability to be a Chairman.

Also to be kept in the Minutes Book at all times should be a copy of the Articles of Incorporation if the organization is a corporate body. A few extra copies of this document should also be on hand.

APPENDIX

Sample of Minutes*

Minutes of a Regular Meeting
of the
Idyll Glen Garden Club

HELD SATURDAY, September 24, 1977 at the Club House, 214 West Main St., Idyll Glen, California, called for 2:00 P.M.

Present: Rose Miller, President and Chairman, Alfred Jordan, Treasurer, Ann Walters, Secretary, four members of the Advisory Committee, and twenty-six other members.

Also Present by invitation: Ralph Proctor, City Councilman, Betty Frost, reporter from the *Idyll Glen News,* and Mr. and Mrs. George Rasmussen of Colorado, guests of Mrs. Miller.

Absent: Ethel Barker, Vice President (traveling), Daniel Gross, Chairman of the Advisory Committee (ill).

The meeting was called to order at 2:07 P.M. by the Chairman.

MINUTES OF The minutes of the meeting of August
LAST MEETING 27 were read by the Secretary. Upon motion of Alan Smith, seconded by Dorothy Gonzales and unanimously passed, it was
RESOLVED that the minutes of August 27, 1977, be, and they hereby are, approved as read.

TREASURER'S Mr. Jordan gave a brief summary of
REPORT the financial activities of the Club since the last meeting and reminded those who have not already done so to pay their dues for the current

---

*Any similarities of names used in this book and living persons or actual places are purely coincidental and unintentional; all illustrations and examples are fictional.

fiscal year. Upon motion of Alice Bell, seconded by Edward West and unanimously passed, it was

RESOLVED that the Treasurer's report be, and it hereby is, approved as read.

Initial plans for the Annual Chrysan-   **MUM**
themum Show were discussed in fur-   **SHOW**
ther detail. The Chairman appointed
Esther and John Altman as Co-Chairpersons of a committee to take care of the physical arrangements for the display, suggesting that volunteers who wish to help get in touch with Mr. and Mrs. Altman. The Chairman also appointed Gladys Baker to be in charge of publicity for the event.

Gloria Johnson reported that due to   **BULLETIN**
absence or illness of several persons,   **BOARD CARE**
the routine care of the Bulletin Board
next to the Post Office has deteriorated lately and that she would welcome a few volunteers who would undertake to refill the vases and clear the notices at certain regular times. Several persons offered to help and were requested by the Chairman to get in touch with Mrs. Johnson.

The Chairman introduced Councilman   **FOUNTAIN**
Proctor who had been invited to be   **IN PARK**
present at this meeting. Mr. Proctor
stated that, as was already well known, funds had been donated to the City to construct a fountain at the entrance to the City Center Park on Main Street, and that the Council would be glad if the Garden Club would undertake to design the landscaping around the fountain and in the near vicinity. He also stated that a modest sum was available to cover costs of a professional plot plan and perspective drawings, but that donations of plants would be grate- fully received. Those present expressed much interest and after discussion and questions answered by Mr. Proctor, the Chairman appointed Architect Alexander Wiley to head a committee of three to co-ordinate the many suggestions of the members and to formulate a plan. He was asked to choose the two other commit- tee members who were to work with him.

TREE COMMITTEE   Mrs. Gulliver, Chairwoman of the Tree Protection Committee, was asked for a progress report. She stated that recent activities of the committee related to contacting the Public Works Department for the purpose of having more satisfactory bumpers installed around trees at the edge of the streets which are subject to damage from cars being parked. She stated that a little progress had been made and that further improvements had been promised as soon as funds could be made available.

NEXT MEETING   The time for the next meeting was
OCTOBER 22   fixed for Saturday, October 22, at 2:00 P.M. at the Club House.

The Chairman announced that after this meeting, light refreshments would be served by Mesdames Jewell and Abernathy.

There being no further business, upon motion of Mr. West, seconded by Miss Carter and unanimously passed, it was
RESOLVED that the meeting be adjourned.

The meeting was closed at 4:38 P.M.

(Signature)
_____
Chairman

(Signature)
_____
Secretary